Wear Your Art

Contents

Wearable

Written by Andrew Polson   Photographed by Craig Potton

Have you ever heard
of art you can wear?
It's not a painting.
It's not a sculpture.
It's a bit like a costume.
It's called wearable art.

People make wearable art from almost anything!
Some people use fabric.
Some people use old toys.
Some people use paper, shells,
and feathers.
Some people even use car parts
such as bumpers!

Every year, there is a show
for this kind of art.
An artist named
Suzie Moncrieff
started the show in 1987.
The show is held
in a sports stadium.
Inside, there is a big stage.
It's called a catwalk.
Nearly two hundred pieces
of wearable art come down the catwalk.

Where did
the word catwalk
come from?

Music, lighting, and special effects
help make the show exciting.
The show lasts for three nights.
About 2,600 people see the show
each night.
Judges look at the pieces carefully.
At the end, the best pieces
win prizes.

5

Today, people
from all over the world
come to see the show.
They want to see
the unusual artworks
up close.

This piece is called
Rainbow Warrior.
It is made of
painted sailcloth
and shade mesh.

This piece is called *Sunyama*. It is made of plastic foam.

This piece is called *Glories of a Garage Sale*. It is made of beads stuck on a black suit.

This piece is called
Total Recall.
It is made of
telephones.

This piece is
called *Wired*.
It is made of
stainless steel.

What materials
would you use to make
a wearable art
costume?

9

Bringing Art

Written by Andrew Polson

Annemiek Weterings
is an artist.
She makes
wearable art.

Q. How did you start making wearable art?

A. I started by painting faces on cloth.
I made these into clothes.
This led to making wearable art.

Q. What do you like about this kind of art?

A. I like it that people can put on my artwork.
It makes the art come to life!

to Life

What would you use to make this tree costume?

Q. Where do you get your ideas?

A. My ideas come from trees, plants, insects, and animals. I also get ideas from people's faces.

A. First, I get an idea.
I do a drawing of how I want it to look.
I do more drawings
to help me think how to make it.

The next step is different for each piece.
For this character, I made a model
out of wood, newspaper, and string.
I built the costume onto it.
Then I made a harness
for the person wearing the costume.
(The harness keeps the costume in place.)
I made a metal frame for the head.
Then I put fabric
over the top.

1

Q. Tell us about this artwork,
Imaginary Friends.

A. I made this with my friend Chris Covich.
Chris and I made up a story
about two friends walking together.
We found a girl named Zeta
who wanted to wear the costume.
We told Zeta the story.
She put the mask on
and made the story come to life!
When the crazy waddling guy fell over
or went the wrong way,
she would pick him up, cuddle him,
and signal for him to come along.
Then she would point
and laugh at the audience.

This is a hard costume to wear.
We were lucky to have
such a great actor
to make it come to life.

How would you react if you were in the audience?

Q. How do you get into the wearable art show?

A. Anyone can enter artworks for the show.
About two hundred pieces are chosen each year.
Don't give up if your work doesn't get in
the first time.
There are different judges every year
and your work will get better every year.

1

2

This is Hughmis M. Shroom.
In 2000, he won the children's section of the show.
His eyes move from side to side.
It was hard to work out how to move the eyes.

What sort of story do you think Hughmis M. Shroom would star in?

3

A. Because it's a great show.

I have entered it six times.

It takes all my energy to think up a new idea.

But I love being a part of the show.

A Change of Face

Written by Angie Belcher
Illustrated by Sandra Cammell

Ella and Jamie sat on Ella's porch.
"There's nothing to do," grumbled Jamie.

"Let's go to the fair," said Ella.
"We can get our faces painted!"

"No. We don't have any money," moaned Jamie.

"I know!" said Ella.
"Let's paint our own faces!"

"Can you face paint?" asked Jamie.

"Sure," said Ella.
"It's easy."

Ella found some old paint on a shelf.
"We can use this," she said.

Jamie frowned.
"I don't want you to paint my face."

"OK," said Ella.
"I'll paint your arm!"

Ella took the lid off the paint. "It smells funny," said Jamie.

"That's because it's old," said Ella. She stirred the paint.

"It looks strange," moaned Jamie. Ella spread the paint over his arm.

"It feels sticky!" said Jamie.

Why is it important to read instructions before using things?

Ella dabbed her fingers on his arm.
The paint was still sticky.
She picked up a cloth.
She tried to wipe off some of the paint.
It didn't come off.
"Uh-oh," she said.

"What are we going to do now?" cried Jamie.

Ella thought for a moment.
"Let's ask Mrs. Evans at the costume shop," said Ella.
"Maybe she will help us."

Jamie and Ella ran to the shop.
Mrs. Evans looked at Jamie's arm.
"That paint is not for using on your skin," she said.
"It takes more than water and soap to remove it."
She rubbed some paint remover on Jamie's arm.
Slowly, the paint came off.

"Face painting is fun," said Mrs. Evans.
"But you need to use the right paint.
Come on. I'll show you."

Mrs. Evans put a towel around Ella's neck.
"You must only use water-based face paints."
She covered Ella's face with a white cream.
"This will make it easy to get the paint off," she said.
Then she covered Ella's face with yellow paint.

It wasn't smelly.
It wasn't sticky.
"Be very careful around the eyes," she said.
Mrs. Evans painted and painted.
At last she was done.

Ella looked in the mirror.
She saw a cat.
"Meow!" she said.

"Now it is your turn, Jamie," said Mrs. Evans.

"May I do it?" asked Ella.

"Oh no!" said Jamie.

"Oh yes," said Ella.
"I know just what to do."

Ella rubbed the cream into his face.
She painted and painted.
At last she was done.

What kind of face would you paint?

Jamie looked in the mirror.
He saw a happy clown.
He smiled for the first time all day.
"Wow!" he said.

"Great job," said Mrs. Evans.

"It's easy," said Ella, "once you know how."

25

Hands-On Art

Written by Seema Kumar

January 11

Dear Nikki,

Here I am in India!
It was my cousin Sunita's wedding today.
She married a man named Rakesh.

The day before the wedding,
Sunita had patterns
painted on her hands and feet.
The patterns were made with henna.
Sunita looked very beautiful.

I took some photos to show you.

Write soon,
Rita

In India before a wedding, the women have a party. An artist paints patterns with henna paste on the bride's hands and feet. The henna paste is left on the skin for up to 12 hours. When the paste is taken off, red patterns are left on the skin.

Henna Patte

A funnel filled with henna paste is used to paint the patterns.

Pattern book

Henna powder + Lemon juice + Tea = Henna paste

The bride's henna patterns will last about a month after her wedding.

Mixing henna

Filling funnel

Feet patterns

An Indian pattern

A Moroccan pattern

Another name for *henna* is *mehndi* (*meh HEN dee*).

People have used henna to paint their bodies for thousands of years. Different countries have different henna patterns and use different henna colors. In India and Asia, the henna is usually reddish brown. In Africa, the henna is usually black.

Often the groom will have his hands and feet painted with henna as well.

A Sudanese groom's pattern

An Indian pattern

A Sudanese pattern

Index